THE-A TEAM PRESENTS...

Meet the A-Team

A Book About Autism

Authored by
Courtney Butorac

Illustrations by
Emily Zieroth

Produced by PBL Consulting
936 NW 57th St
Seattle, WA 98107
www.sociallearning.org

Please contact
PBL Consulting at
info@pblconsulting.org
for more information.

MW00902132

Hi! My name is Alex and these are my friends, Lily, Max, Jack and Bella. We are part of Ms. Corina's friendship group.

2

What is autism? Well, my mom explained it to me last year and I will try to explain it to you.

The first thing she told me is that autism is NOT a disease or something you can catch. My mom also said that having autism is NOT something bad, it's just something different. She even explained that some of the greatest inventors, musicians and artists had autism. However, adults and kids with autism may share similar struggles.

You know how when you have a conversation with someone, you look at them, face your body towards them, and talk about the same thing?

A kid with autism might have their body turned away, be looking at something else and talking about their own interest.

This is one of the reasons that making friends can be difficult.

7

Or you know when your mom looks at you with an angry face and their arms crossed and you know they are mad?

Well, a kid with autism might not understand that because they have a hard time reading facial expressions and body language.

Another thing is understanding that people feel differently about things. A kid with autism might think that because pizza is their favorite food, it should be everyone's favorite food! Or if they don't like dogs, no one should like dogs.

9

Also, kids with autism can also have really strong interests in specific areas.

For example, a 3-year-old with autism might know everything about outer space.

That means they can have a hard time thinking and talking about other topics.

Kids with autism aren't always flexible and like things to be the same way all the time. For example, a kid with autism might line up toys in the same way every day.

They also like to know the rules of all situations, and if you aren't following those rules, they might let you know.

12

Some kids with autism
have lots of worries.
This is often because
they don't understand and
can't control what is going on
in their world every day.

Finally, some kids with autism have sensory issues. Let me explain this...

THE FIVE SENSES

TASTE

SIGHT

14

There are five senses right?
Taste, touch, smell, hear, see.

SMELL

TOUCH

HEAR

Some kids with autism might
be too sensitive to one or
more of the five senses,
while other kids might not
be sensitive enough. **15**

Or eye sensitivity... some lights may be too strong or too painful to kids with autism.

17

Some kids with autism are extra
sensitive to touch and may not like
wearing scratchy clothing or being
touched by others. Even a tag on their
shirt might feel unbearable.

Yet, some kids may not be
so sensitive to touch.

For those kids,
if they fall down
and are bleeding,
they may not
even know it.

CHARACTER SELECT: BELLA

VERBAL COMMUNICATION

NON-VERBAL COMMUNICATION

COGNITION

SOCIAL AWARENESS

FLEXIBILITY

SENSORY

The thing about autism is that it is a spectrum disorder, which means that no one with autism is the same.

Some people say, "if you know ONE kid with autism, then you know ONE kid with autism."

Even though kids with autism share some challenges, they are all unique.

CHARACTER SELECT: ALEX

VERBAL COMMUNICATION

NON-VERBAL COMMUNICATION

COGNITION

SOCIAL AWARENESS

FLEXIBILITY

SENSORY

CHARACTER SELECT:
JACK

VERBAL COMMUNICATION

NON-VERBAL COMMUNICATION

COGNITION

SOCIAL AWARENESS

FLEXIBILITY

SENSORY

CHARACTER SELECT:
LILY

VERBAL COMMUNICATION

NON-VERBAL COMMUNICATION

COGNITION

SOCIAL AWARENESS

FLEXIBILITY

SENSORY

CHARACTER SELECT:
MAX

VERBAL COMMUNICATION

NON-VERBAL COMMUNICATION

COGNITION

SOCIAL AWARENESS

FLEXIBILITY

SENSORY

21

So, my friends and I
all have autism, but
we are all really different.

22

For example, I am really good at sports and facts. I do really well in class and always get good grades. I'm even in advanced classes! I like to be the best at what I do, which sometimes gets me in trouble.

I don't like losing. I mean, I really, really don't like to lose. My mom also says I have a hard time compromising, and I'm not really good at letting other people be in charge. But the hardest thing for me is controlling my temper.

25

Max knows everything about cars. He is super skilled in math, however both reading and writing are hard for him. Sometimes, it's difficult for Max to have a conversation with others because he often goes back to talking about cars while we are having a conversation about something else. This can be frustrating for other kids.

Lily does really well in school.

She is a great artist and can draw anything! Like me, Lily can be bossy and likes to be in charge. She also talks back to the teacher and her parents a lot. This can get her into trouble sometimes.

Jack knows everything there is to know about outer space. He is really funny. Sometimes, he gets into trouble at school because he is always making jokes in class. When he's doing that, he's not paying attention to the teacher and misses instructions.
When he gets too silly, it can annoy other kids because they can't get their work done.

Bella is an amazing musician and really shines when she is playing her flute! She is usually quiet and doesn't really get in trouble. But, she feels worried a lot. She gets uncomfortable when other people aren't following the rules or are getting in trouble.

It's also hard for her to be around a lot of noise and so she gets upset when things get too loud.

As you can see, we are all different, but what we have in common is that we are all awesome and have autism.

We have a friendship group a few times a week with our teacher Ms. Corina. In friendship group, we learn ways to make friends and do well in school. The best part is we get a Top Secret Mission each week. If we complete our mission, it means we learned a new skill!

We are always excited to find out about our top secret missions to help us practice important skills.

I wonder what the next one will be...

Expert Endorsement

Ilene S. Schwartz, Ph.D., BCBA-D
University of Washington
Professor of Special Education
Director, Haring Center for Inclusive Education

"Currently 1 in 68 children in the United States is diagnosed with Autism Spectrum Disorder (ASD), a life-long neurodevelopmental disorder.

"Currently 1 in 68 children in the United States is diagnosed with Autism Spectrum Disorder (ASD)..."

That means that almost every child in the US attends school with a peer with ASD, attends an extra-curricular (e.g., Scouts or sports) with a child with ASD, or attends religious school with a child with ASD.

"...almost every child in the US attends school with a peer with ASD..."

Although the prevalence of ASD has increased dramatically over the last 20 years, knowledge about ASD in the general public has not.

"Many adults, including teachers, do not have accurate knowledge about ASD and have unrealistic expectations (and often fears) about children with ASD."

Helping adults learn more about ASD and providing them with appropriate information to share with children is an important first step in creating a society that values, supports, and respects people with ASD and other disabilities.

Meet the A-Team is a lovely book for children and adults that explains ASD in a manner that is accurate, interesting, and engaging. While providing information about ASD, Ms. Butorac introduces us to five children with ASD who bring their individual strengths, areas of need, preferences, and quirks with them to school every day. These children help all of learn more about what ASD is and how it affects children at school and in the community. I am so happy to meet the A-Team and I look forward to sharing this book with my students and their families."

"I look forward to sharing this book with my students and their families."

ABOUT THE AUTHOR

Courtney Butorac

Courtney Butorac has been supporting kids and adults with autism and also their families for 25 years as an elementary school special education teacher, preschool teacher, camp counselor and behavioral therapist. She has pioneered new ways to support social learning within her school district and is an enthusiastic member of a behavior and autism intervention team that engages district-wide to help teachers develop the knowledge and tools to support students with autism in their classrooms. Courtney has designed and facilitated powerful professional learning for educators that focuses on how to teach social skills to students with a broad range of disabilities and how to support behavioral needs in the classroom. Additionally, Courtney has guest lectured multiple times at the University of Washington's early childhood special education program.

Years ago, she and a group of her students with autism formed the A-Team friendship group to tackle the common social challenges facing her kids. These students helped inspire the "The A-Team Presents..." characters and book series.

Courtney has both a Master's Degree in early childhood special education and her Board Certification in Behavior Analysis (BCBA).

Courtney lives in Seattle with her husband, who is a fellow educator, and two young and energetic sons.

Explore more books about various social challenges in "The A-Team" book series!

Find useful, free resources on the web at sociallearning.org

THE A-TEAM PRESENTS...

Bella Gets Worried

A Book About Dealing With Anxiety

Courtney Butorac

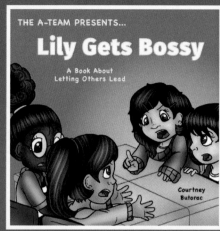

THE A-TEAM PRESENTS...

Lily Gets Bossy

A Book About Letting Others Lead

Courtney Butorac

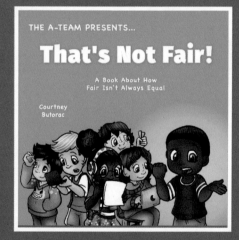

THE A-TEAM PRESENTS...

That's Not Fair!

A Book About How Fair Isn't Always Equal

Courtney Butorac

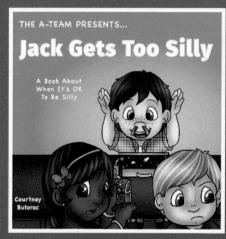

THE A-TEAM PRESENTS...

Jack Gets Too Silly

A Book About When It's OK To Be Silly

Courtney Butorac

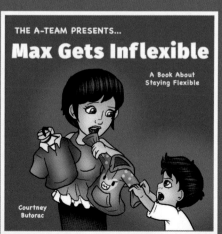

THE A-TEAM PRESENTS...

Max Gets Inflexible

A Book About Staying Flexible

Courtney Butorac

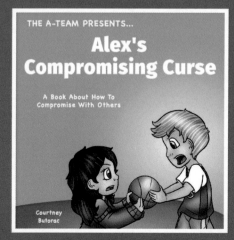

THE A-TEAM PRESENTS...

Alex's Compromising Curse

A Book About How To Compromise With Others

Courtney Butorac